TACITUS

NERO AND THE BURNING OF ROME

TRANSLATED BY MICHAEL GRANT

PENGUIN BOOKS

PENGUIN BOOKS

Published by the Penguin Group
Penguin Books Ltd, 27 Wrights Lane, London w8 5tz, England
Penguin Books USA Inc., 375 Hudson Street, New York, New York 10014, USA
Penguin Books Australia Ltd, Ringwood, Victoria, Australia
Penguin Books Canada Ltd, 10 Alcorn Avenue, Toronto, Ontario, Canada m4v 3b2
Penguin Books (NZ) Ltd, 182–190 Wairau Road, Auckland 10, New Zealand

Penguin Books Ltd, Registered Offices: Harmondsworth, Middlesex, England

These extracts are from Michael Grant's translation of *The Annals of Imperial Rome*
by Tacitus, first published in Penguin Classics 1956; reprinted with revisions 1959,
1971, 1973, 1975
This edition published 1995
1 3 5 7 9 10 8 6 4 2

Translation copyright © Michael Grant Publications Ltd, 1956,
1959, 1971, 1973, 1975
All rights reserved

Printed in England by Clays Ltd, St Ives plc

CONTENTS

Nero and His Helpers

The situation of the country was deteriorating every day; and a counteracting influence now vanished, with the death of Burrus. Whether natural causes or poison killed him is uncertain. The gradually increasing tumour in his throat, which blocked the passage and stopped his breathing, suggested natural causes. But the general view was that Nero, ostensibly proposing a medical treatment, had instructed that Burrus' throat should be painted with a poisonous drug. The patient, it was said, had detected the crime, and when the emperor visited him had turned his face away and only answered Nero's inquiries with the words: '*I am doing all right.*'

The death of Burrus caused great public distress. His merits were dwelt on – also the inferiority of his successors, one harmless but ineffective and the other a notorious criminal. For the emperor now appointed two commanders of the Guard – Faenius Rufus because he was popular (having managed the corn supply without personal profit), and Gaius Ofonius Tigellinus because

Nero found his unending immoralities and evil reputation fascinating. Each commander behaved as expected. Tigellinus was the more influential with the emperor, in whose private debaucheries he participated. Rufus was liked by Guardsmen and civilians: which went against him with Nero.

Burrus' death undermined the influence of Seneca. Decent standards carried less weight when one of their two advocates was gone. Now Nero listened to more disreputable advisers. These attacked Seneca, first for his wealth, which was enormous and excessive for any subject, they said, and was still increasing; secondly, for the grandeur of his mansions and beauty of his gardens, which outdid even the emperor's; and thirdly, for his alleged bid for popularity. They also charged Seneca with allowing no one to be called eloquent but himself. 'He is always writing poetry,' they suggested, 'now that Nero has become fond of it. He openly disparages the emperor's amusements, underestimates him as a charioteer, and makes fun of his singing. How long must merit at Rome be conferred by Seneca's certificate alone? Surely Nero is a boy no longer! He is a grown man and ought to discharge his tutor. His ancestors will teach him all he needs.' Seneca knew of these attacks. People who still had some decency told him of them. Nero increasingly avoided his company.

Seneca, however, requested an audience, and when it was granted, this was what he said. 'It is nearly fourteen years, Caesar, since I became associated with your rising fortunes, eight since you became emperor. During that time you have showered on me such distinctions and riches that, if only I could retire to enjoy them unpretentiously, my prosperity would be complete.

'May I quote illustrious precedents drawn from your rank, not mine? Your great-great-grandfather Augustus allowed Marcus Agrippa to withdraw to Mytilene, and allowed Gaius Maecenas the equivalent of retirement at Rome itself. The one his partner in wars, the other the bearer of many anxious burdens at Rome, they were greatly rewarded, for great services. I have had no claim on your generosity, except my learning. Though acquired outside the glare of public life, it has brought me the wonderful recompense and distinction of having assisted in your early education.

'But you have also bestowed on me measureless favours, and boundless wealth. Accordingly, I often ask myself: "Is it I, son of a provincial knight, who am accounted a national leader? Is mine the unknown name which has come to glitter among the ancient and glorious pedigrees? Where is my old self, that was content with so little? Laying out these fine gardens? Grandly inspecting these estates? Wallowing in my vast revenues?" I can only find one excuse. It was not for me to obstruct your munificence.

'But we have both filled the measure – you, of what an emperor can give his friend, and I, of what a friend may receive from his emperor. Anything more will breed envy. Your greatness is far above all such mortal things. But I am not; so I crave your help. If, in the field or on a journey, I were tired, I should want a stick. In my life's journey, I need just such a support.

'For I am old and cannot do the lightest work. I am no longer equal to the burden of my wealth. Order your agents to take over my property and incorporate it in yours. I do not suggest plunging myself into poverty, but giving up the things that are too brilliant and dazzle me. The time now spent on gardens and mansions shall be devoted to the mind. You have abundant strength. For years the supreme power has been familiar to you. We older friends may ask for our rest. This, too, will add to your glory – that you have raised to the heights men content with lower positions.'

The substance of Nero's reply was this. 'My first debt to you is that I can reply impromptu to your premeditated speech. For you taught me to improvise as well as to make prepared orations. True, my great-great-grandfather Augustus permitted Agrippa and Maecenas to rest after their labours. But he did so when he was old enough to assure them, by his prestige, of everything – of whatever kind – that he had given them. Besides, he certainly deprived neither of the rewards which they earned from him in the wars and crises of Augustus' youthful years. If my life had been warlike, you too would have fought for me. But you gave what your situation demanded: wisdom, advice, philosophy, to support me as a boy and as a youth. Your gifts to me will endure as long as life itself! My gifts to you, gardens and mansions and revenues, are liable to circumstances.

'They may seem extensive. But many people far less deserving than you have had more. I omit, from shame, to mention ex-slaves who flaunt greater wealth. I am even ashamed that you, my dearest friend, are not the richest of all men. You are still vigorous and fit for State affairs and their rewards. My reign is only beginning. Or do you think you have reached your limit? If so you must rank yourself below Lucius Vitellius, thrice consul, and my generosity below that of Claudius, and my gifts as inferior to the lifelong savings of Lucius Volusius Saturninus (II).

'If youth's slippery paths lead me astray, be at hand to call me back! You equipped my manhood; devote even greater care to guiding it! If you return my gifts and desert your emperor, it is not your unpretentiousness, your retirement, that will be on everyone's lips, but *my* meanness, your dread of *my* brutality. However much your self-denial were praised, no philosopher could becomingly gain credit from an action damaging to his friend's reputation.'

Then he clasped and kissed Seneca. Nature and experience had fitted Nero to conceal hatred behind treacherous embraces. Seneca expressed his gratitude (all conversations with autocrats end like that). But he abandoned the customs of his former ascendancy. Terminating his large receptions, he dismissed his entourage, and rarely visited Rome. Ill-health or philosophical studies kept him at home, he said.

After Seneca's elimination it was easy to bring down the commander of the Guard Faenius Rufus, who was accused of friendship with Agrippina. Faenius' colleague

Tigellinus became more powerful every day. But he felt that his criminal aptitudes – the only qualities he possessed – would influence the emperor more if he could make them partners in crime. Studying Nero's fears, Tigellinus found he chiefly dreaded Rubellius Plautus and Faustus Cornelius Sulla Felix. One had been recently removed to Asia, the other to southern Gaul. Tigellinus enlarged on their aristocratic origins, and their present proximity to the armies of the east and of Germany respectively.

'I have no divided allegiance like Burrus,' he said. 'My only thought is your safety! At Rome this may in some degree be ensured by vigilance on the spot. But how can one suppress sedition far away? The dictator Sulla's name has excited the Gauls. For the peoples of Asia Drusus' grandson is just as unsettling. Sulla's poverty increases his daring. He pretends to be lazy – yet he is only biding his time for a *coup*. Plautus is rich, and does not pretend to like retirement. He parades an admiration of the ancient Romans, but he has the arrogance of the Stoics, who breed sedition and intrigue.'

Action was not long delayed. Five days later, Sulla was murdered at dinner. Assassins had reached Massilia before the alarm. His head was transported to Nero, who joked that it was disfigured by premature greyness.

The plans for Plautus' death were less secret. More people were interested in his safety. Besides, the length and duration of the land and sea journeys encouraged rumours. The story was invented that Plautus had escaped to Corbulo who, having mighty armies behind him, would be in the gravest peril if there was to be a massacre of blameless notables. Asia, it was said, had risen in Plautus' support; the few, unenthusiastic, soldiers sent to murder him had failed to carry out their orders and had joined the rebellion. Idle credulity, as usual, amplified these fictitious rumours.

Meanwhile an ex-slave of Plautus, helped by favourable winds, outstripped the staff-officer of the Guard who had been sent against him, and brought a message from Plautus' father-in-law, Lucius Antistius Vetus. 'Escape a passive end while there is a way out!' advised Antistius. 'Sympathy for your great name will make decent men back you and brave men help you. Meantime, disdain no possible support. Sixty soldiers have been sent. If you can repulse them, much can happen – even a war can develop – before Nero receives the news and sends another force. In short, either you save yourself by this action, or at least a bold end is as good as a timid one.'

But Plautus remained unimpressed. Either he felt helpless – an unarmed exile – or the suspense wearied him. Or perhaps he believed that his wife and children, whom he loved, would be the more leniently treated if the emperor were not upset by an alarm. One account states that his father-in-law sent further messages saying that Plautus was in no danger. Or his philosophical friends, the Greek Coeranus and the Etruscan Gaius Musonius Rufus, may have recommended an imperturbable death rather than a hazardous, anxious life.

The killers found him at midday, stripped for exercise. Supervised by the eunuch Pelago whom Nero had put in charge of the gang – like a slave set over a monarch's underlings – the officer slew him as he was. The victim's head was brought to Nero. I will quote the actual words he uttered when he saw it. 'Nero,' he said, 'how could such a long-nosed man have frightened you?'

Indeed, the fears which had caused the emperor to postpone his wedding with Poppaea were now dispelled. He planned to marry her quickly, after eliminating Octavia, his wife. Octavia's conduct was unassuming; but he hated her, because she was popular and an emperor's daughter. First Nero wrote to the senate emphasizing his personal solicitude for the national interests, and – without admitting their murder – denouncing Sulla and Plautus as agitators. On these grounds the senate voted a thanksgiving, and the two men's expulsion from the senate. This was a mockery which caused greater disgust even than the crimes. Hearing of their decree, Nero concluded that all his misdeeds were accounted meritorious. So he divorced Octavia for barrenness, and married Poppaea.

Dominating Nero as his wife, as she had long dominated him as his mistress, Poppaea incited one of Octavia's household to accuse Octavia of adultery with a slave – an Alexandrian flute-player called Eucaerus was designated for the role. Octavia's maids were tortured, and though some were induced by the pain to make false confessions, the majority unflinchingly maintained her innocence. One retorted that the mouth of Tigellinus, who was bullying her, was less clean than any part of Octavia. Nevertheless, she was put away. First, there was an ordinary divorce: she received the ominous gifts of Burrus' house and Rubellius Plautus' estates. Soon, however, she was banished to Campania, under military surveillance.

Now indiscretion is safer for the Roman public than for their superiors, since they are insignificant; and they protested openly and loudly. This seemed to recall Nero to decency, and he proposed to make Octavia his wife again. Happy crowds climbed the Capitol, thankful to heaven at last. They overturned Poppaea's statues and carried Octavia's on their shoulders, showering flowers on them and setting them in the Forum and temples.

Even the emperor was acclaimed and worshipped again. Indeed a noisy crowd invaded the palace. But detachments of troops clubbed them and forced them back at the point of the sword. Then the changes the rioters had inspired were reversed, and Poppaea reinstated. Always a savage hater, she was now mad with fear of mass violence and Nero's capitulation to it. She fell at his feet crying: 'Now that things have reached this pass, it is not marriage I am fighting for, but what, to me, means less than my marriage – my life. It is in danger from Octavia's dependants and slaves! They pretend to be the people of Rome! They commit, in peace-time, outrages that could hardly happen even in war! The emperor is their target – they only lack a leader. And once disorders begin one will easily be found, when she leaves Campania and proceeds to the capital! Even her distant nod causes riots.

'What have *I* done wrong? Whom have I injured? Or is all this because I am going to give an authentic heir to the house of the Caesars? Would Rome prefer an Egyptian flute-player's child to be introduced into the palace? If you think it is best, take back your directress voluntarily – do not be coerced into doing so. Or else, safeguard yourself! Punish suitably. No severity was needed to end the first troubles. Besides, once they lose hope of Nero keeping Octavia, they will find her another husband.'

Popaea's arguments, playing on Nero's alarm and anger in turn, duly terrified and infuriated him. But the suspicions concerning Octavia's slave came to nothing; the examination of her servants proved fruitless. So it was decided to extract a confession of adultery from someone against whom a charge of revolution could also be concocted. A suitable person seemed to be Anicetus, fleet-commander at Misenum and instrument of Nero's matricide. After the crime he had been fairly well regarded. Later, however, he was in serious disfavour; for the sight of a former accomplice in terrible crimes is a reproach.

Nero summoned him, and reminded him of his previous job – Anicetus alone had protected his emperor against his mother's plotting. Now, said Nero, he could earn equal gratitude by eliminating a detested wife. No violence or weapons were needed. Anicetus only had to confess adultery with Octavia. Great rewards were promised – though at present they were unspecified – and an agreed place of retirement. Refusal would mean death. Anicetus' warped character found no difficulty in a further crime. Indeed, the confession which he made to Nero's friends, assembled as a council of state, even exceeded his instructions. Then he was removed to comfortable exile in Sardinia, where he died a natural death.

Nero reported in an edict that Octavia had tried to win over the fleet by seducing its commander, and then, nervous about her unfaithfulness, had procured an abortion (the emperor forgot his recent charge of sterility). She was then confined on the island of Pandateria.

No exiled woman ever earned greater sympathy from those who saw her. Some still remembered the banishment of the elder Agrippina by Tiberius and, more recently, of Julia Livilla by Claudius. Yet they had been mature women with happy memories which could alleviate their present sufferings. But Octavia had virtually died on her wedding day. Her new home had brought her nothing but misery. Poison had removed her father, and very soon her brother. Maid had been preferred to mistress. Then she, Nero's wife, had been ruined by her successor. Last came the bitterest of all fates, this accusation.

So this girl, in her twentieth year, was picketed by company-commanders of the Guard and their men. She was hardly a living person any more – so certain was she of imminent destruction. Yet still she lacked the peace of death. The order to die arrived a few days later. She protested that she was a wife no longer – Nero's sister only. She invoked the Germanici, the relations she shared with Nero. Finally she even invoked Agrippina, in whose days her marriage had been unhappy, certainly, but at least not fatal. But Octavia was bound, and all her veins were opened. However, her terror retarded the flow of blood. So she was put into an exceedingly hot vapour-bath and suffocated. An even crueller atrocity followed. Her head was cut off and taken to Rome for Poppaea to see.

How long must I go on recording the thank-offerings in temples on such occasions? Every reader about that epoch, in my own work or others, can assume that the gods were thanked every time the emperor ordered a banishment or murder; and, conversely, that happenings once regarded joyfully were now treated as national disasters. Nevertheless, when any senatorial decree reaches new depths of sycophancy or abasement, I will not leave it unrecorded.

In the same year Nero was believed to have poisoned two of his most prominent ex-slaves – Doryphorus for opposing the emperor's marriage with Poppaea, and Pallas for reserving his own immense riches for himself by living so long.

Seneca was secretly denounced by Romanus as an associate of Gaius Calpurnius Piso. But Seneca more effectively turned the same charge against his accuser. However, the incident alarmed Piso – and by so doing initiated a far-reaching, disastrous conspiracy against Nero.

The Burning of Rome

When the new year [AD 64] began, with Gaius Laecanius Bassus and Marcus Licinius Crassus Frugi (II) as consuls, Nero showed daily-increasing impatience to appear regularly on the public stage. Hitherto, he had sung at home, or at the Youth Games held in his Gardens. But he began to disdain such occasions as insufficiently attended and too restricted for a voice like his. Not venturing, however, to make his début at Rome, he selected Neapolis, as being a Greek city. Starting there, he planned to cross to Greece, win the glorious and long-revered wreaths of its Games, and thus increase his fame and popularity at home.

The Neapolitan theatre was filled. Besides the local population, it contained visitors from all around attracted by the notable occasion. Present, too, were those who attended the emperor out of respect or to perform various services — and even units of his troops. The theatre now provided what seemed to most people an evil omen, but to Nero a sign of divine providence and favour. For when it was empty (the crowd having left), it collapsed. But there were no casualties; and Nero composed a poem thanking the gods for the happy outcome of the incident.

Then, on his way to cross the Adriatic, he stopped for a while at Beneventum. There large crowds were attending a gladiatorial display given by a certain Vatinius. This outstanding monstrosity of the court had originated from a shoe shop. Deformed in body and scurrilous in wit, he had first been taken up as a butt for abuse. But then he gained power enough to eclipse any scoundrel in influence, wealth, and capacity for damage. He rose by attacking decent people.

But even at his pleasures, attending this man's show, Nero took no vacation from crime. For enforced death now came to Decimus Junius Silanus Torquatus. This was because, in addition to the nobility of his Junian house, he could claim the divine Augustus as a great-great-grandfather. The accusers were instructed to charge Torquatus with generosity so extravagant that revolution had become his only hope. Censure was also to be directed against the titles which he gave some of his former slaves – Secretary-General, Petitions Secretary, and Financial Secretary. These, it was alleged, were the titles of an imperial household: Torquatus must be preparing for one. His confidential ex-slaves were arrested and removed. Seeing conviction ahead, he opened his veins. Nero made the usual pronouncement indicating that, however guilty and rightly distrustful of his defence Torquatus had been, he would nevertheless – if he had awaited his judge's mercy – have lived.

Before long Nero, for some reason unknown, postponed his visit to Greece, and returned to Rome. But he still planned to visit the eastern provinces, particularly Egypt; and his secret thoughts dwelt on them. After announcing by edict that his absence would be brief and all branches of government would carry on with undiminished efficiency, he proceeded to the Capitol for consultation about his journey. After worshipping the Capitoline gods, he entered the shrine of Vesta. But there all his limbs suddenly began to tremble. The goddess frightened him. Or perhaps he was always frightened, remembering his crimes. At all events, he abandoned this journey too.

His patriotism came before everything, Nero asserted; he had seen the people's sad faces and heard their private lamentations about the extensive travels he planned – even his brief absences they found unendurable, being accustomed (he added) to derive comfort in life's misfortunes from the sight of their emperor. Just as in private relationships nearest are dearest, he said, so to him the inhabitants of Rome came first: he must obey their appeal to stay! The people liked such protestations. They loved their amusements. But their principal interest was the corn supply: and they feared it would run short if Nero went away. Senators and leading men were uncertain whether he was more abominable present or absent. Subsequently, as happens when men undergo terrifying experiences, the alternative that had befallen them seemed the graver.

Nero himself now tried to make it appear that Rome was his favourite abode. He gave feasts in public places as if the whole city were his own home. But the most prodigal and notorious banquet was given by Tigellinus. To avoid repetitious accounts of extravagance, I shall describe it, as a model of its kind. The entertainment took place on a raft constructed on Marcus Agrippa's lake. It was towed about by other vessels, with gold and ivory fittings. Their rowers were degenerates, assorted according to age and vice. Tigellinus had also collected birds and animals from remote countries, and even the products of the ocean. On the quays were brothels stocked with high-ranking ladies. Opposite them could be seen naked prostitutes, indecently posturing and gesturing.

At nightfall the woods and houses nearby echoed with singing and blazed with lights. Nero was already corrupted by every lust, natural and unnatural. But now he refuted any surmises that no further degradation was possible for him. For a few days later he went through a formal wedding ceremony with one of the perverted gang called Pythagoras. The emperor, in the presence of witnesses, put on the bridal veil. Dowry, marriage bed, wedding torches, all were there. Indeed everything was public which even in a natural union is veiled by night.

Disaster followed. Whether it was accidental or caused by a criminal act on the part of the emperor is uncertain – both versions have supporters. Now started the most terrible and destructive fire which Rome had ever experienced. It began in the Circus, where it adjoins the Palatine and Caelian hills. Breaking out in shops selling inflammable goods, and fanned by the wind, the conflagration instantly grew and swept the whole length of the Circus. There were no walled mansions or temples, or any other obstructions, which could arrest it. First, the fire swept violently over the level spaces. Then it climbed the hills – but returned to ravage the lower ground again. It outstripped every counter-measure. The ancient city's narrow winding streets and irregular blocks encouraged its progress.

Terrified, shrieking women, helpless old and young, people intent on their own safety, people unselfishly supporting invalids or waiting for them, fugitives and lingerers alike – all heightened the confusion. When people looked back, menacing flames sprang up before them or outflanked them. When they escaped to a neighbouring quarter, the fire followed – even districts believed remote proved to be involved. Finally, with no idea where or what to flee, they crowded on to the country roads, or lay in the fields. Some who had lost everything – even their food for the day – could have escaped, but preferred to die. So did others, who had failed to rescue their loved ones. Nobody dared fight the flames. Attempts to do so were prevented by menac-ing gangs. Torches, too, were openly thrown in, by men crying that they acted under orders. Perhaps they had received orders. Or they may just have wanted to plun-der unhampered.

Nero was at Antium. He only returned to the city

when the fire was approaching the mansion he had built to link the Gardens of Maecenas to the Palatine. The flames could not be prevented from overwhelming the whole of the Palatine, including his palace. Nevertheless, for the relief of the homeless, fugitive masses he threw open the Field of Mars, including Agrippa's public buildings, and even his own Gardens. Nero also constructed emergency accommodation for the destitute multitude. Food was brought from Ostia and neighbouring towns, and the price of corn was cut to less than $\frac{1}{4}$ sesterce a pound. Yet these measures, for all their popular character, earned no gratitude. For a rumour had spread that, while the city was burning, Nero had gone to his private stage and, comparing modern calamities with ancient, had sung of the destruction of Troy.

By the sixth day enormous demolitions had confronted the raging flames with bare ground and open sky, and the fire was finally stamped out at the foot of the Esquiline Hill. But before panic had subsided, or hope revived, flames broke out again in the more open regions of the city. Here there were fewer casualties; but the destruction of temples and pleasure arcades was even worse. This new conflagration caused additional ill-feeling because it started on Tigellinus' estate in the

Aemilian district. For people believed that Nero was ambitious to found a new city to be called after himself.

Of Rome's fourteen districts only four remained intact. Three were levelled to the ground. The other seven were reduced to a few scorched and mangled ruins. To count the mansions, blocks, and temples destroyed would be difficult. They included shrines of remote antiquity, such as Servius Tullius' temple of the Moon, the Great Altar and holy place dedicated by Evander to Hercules, the temple vowed by Romulus to Jupiter the Stayer, Numa's sacred residence, and Vesta's shrine containing Rome's household gods. Among the losses, too, were the precious spoils of countless victories, Greek artistic masterpieces, and authentic records of old Roman genius. All the splendour of the rebuilt city did not prevent the older generation from remembering these irreplaceable objects. It was noted that the fire had started on July 19th, the day on which the Senonian Gauls had captured and burnt the city. Others elaborately calculated that the two fires were separated by the same number of years, months, and days.

But Nero profited by his country's ruin to build a new palace. Its wonders were not so much customary and commonplace luxuries like gold and jewels, but lawns and lakes and faked rusticity – woods here, open spaces and views there. With their cunning, impudent artificialities, Nero's architects and engineers, Severus and Celer, did not balk at effects which Nature herself had ruled out as impossible.

They also fooled away an emperor's riches. For they promised to dig a navigable canal from Lake Avernus to the Tiber estuary, over the stony shore and mountain barriers. The only water to feed the canal was in the Pontine marshes. Elsewhere, all was precipitous or waterless. Moreover, even if a passage could have been forced, the labour would have been unendurable and unjustified. But Nero was eager to perform the incredible; so he attempted to excavate the hills adjoining Lake Avernus. Traces of his frustrated hopes are visible today.

In parts of Rome unfilled by Nero's palace, construction was not – as after the burning by the Gauls – without plan or demarcation. Street-fronts were of regulated dimensions and alignment, streets were broad, and houses spacious. Their height was restricted, and their frontages protected by colonnades. Nero undertook to erect these at his own expense, and also to clear debris from building-sites before transferring them to their owners. He announced bonuses, in proportion to rank and resources, for the completion of houses and blocks before a given date. Rubbish was to be dumped in the Ostian marshes by corn-ships returning down the Tiber.

A fixed proportion of every building had to be massive, untimbered stone from Gabii or Alba (these stones being fireproof). Furthermore, guards were to ensure a more abundant and extensive public water-supply, hitherto diminished by irregular private enterprise. Householders were obliged to keep fire-fighting apparatus in an accessible place; and semi-detached houses were forbidden – they must have their own walls. These measures were welcomed for their practicality, and they beautified the new city. Some, however, believed that the old town's configuration had been healthier, since its narrow streets and high houses had provided protection against the burning sun, whereas now the shadowless open spaces radiated a fiercer heat.

So much for human precautions. Next came attempts to appease heaven. After consultation of the Sibylline books, prayers were addressed to Vulcan, Ceres, and Proserpina. Juno, too, was propitiated. Women who had been married were responsible for the rites – first on the Capitol, then at the nearest sea-board, where water was taken to sprinkle her temple and statue. Women with husbands living also celebrated ritual banquets and vigils.

But neither human resources, nor imperial munificence, nor appeasement of the gods, eliminated sinister suspicions that the fire had been instigated. To suppress this rumour, Nero fabricated scapegoats – and punished with every refinement the notoriously depraved Christians (as they were popularly called). Their originator, Christ, had been executed in Tiberius' reign by the governor of Judaea, Pontius Pilatus. But in spite of this temporary setback the deadly superstition had broken out afresh, not only in Judaea (where the mischief had started) but even in Rome. All degraded and shameful practices collect and flourish in the capital.

First, Nero had self-acknowledged Christians arrested. Then, on their information, large numbers of others were condemned – not so much for incendiarism as for their anti-social tendencies. Their deaths were made farcical. Dressed in wild animals' skins, they were torn to pieces by dogs, or crucified, or made into torches to be ignited after dark as substitutes for daylight. Nero provided his Gardens for the spectacle, and exhibited displays in the Circus, at which he mingled with the crowd – or stood in a chariot, dressed as a charioteer. Despite their guilt as Christians, and the ruthless punishment it deserved, the victims were pitied. For it was felt that they were being sacrificed to one man's brutality rather than to the national interest.

Meanwhile Italy was ransacked for funds, and the provinces were ruined – unprivileged and privileged communities alike. Even the gods were included in the looting. Temples at Rome were robbed, and emptied of the gold dedicated for the triumphs and vows, the ambitions and fears, of generations of Romans. Plunder from Asia and Greece included not only offerings but actual statues of the gods. Two agents were sent to these provinces. One, Acratus, was an ex-slave, capable of any depravity. The other, Secundus Carrinas, professed Greek culture, but no virtue from it percolated to his heart.

Seneca, rumour went, sought to avoid the odium of his sacrilege by asking leave to retire to a distant country retreat, and then – permission being refused – feigning a muscular complaint and keeping to his bedroom. According to some accounts one of his former slaves, Cleonicus by name, acting on Nero's orders intended to poison Seneca but he escaped – either because the man confessed or because Seneca's own fears caused him to live very simply on plain fruit, quenching his thirst with running water.

At this juncture there was an attempted break-out by gladiators at Praeneste. Their army guards overpowered them. But the Roman public, as always terrified (or fascinated) by revolution, were already talking of ancient calamities such as the rising of Spartacus. Soon afterwards a naval disaster occurred. This was not on active service; never had there been such profound peace. But Nero had ordered the fleet to return to Campania by a fixed date regardless of weather. So, despite heavy seas, the steersmen started from Formiae. But when they tried to round Cape Misenum a south-westerly gale drove them ashore near Cumae and destroyed numerous warships and smaller craft.

As the year ended, omens of impending misfortune were widely rumoured – unprecedentedly frequent lightning; a comet (atoned for by Nero, as usual, by aristocratic blood); two-headed offspring of men and beasts, thrown into the streets or discovered among the offerings to those deities to whom pregnant victims are sacrificed. Near Placentia a calf was born beside the road with its head fastened to one of its legs. Soothsayers deduced that a new head was being prepared for the world – but that it would be neither powerful nor secret since it had been deformed in the womb and given birth by the roadside.

The Plot

The consuls for the following year [AD 65] were Aulus
Licinius Nerva Silanus Firmus Pasidienus and Marcus
Julius Vestinus Atticus. As soon as they had assumed
office, a conspiracy was hatched and instantly gained
strength. Senators and knights, officers, even women,
competed to join. They hated Nero; and they liked
Gaius Calpurnius Piso. His membership of the aristocratic Calpurnian house linked him, on his father's side,
with many illustrious families. Among the masses, too,
he enjoyed a great reputation for his good qualities, real
or apparent. For he employed his eloquence to defend
his fellow-citizens in court; he was a generous friend –
and gracious and affable even to strangers; and he also
possessed the accidental advantages of impressive stature
and a handsome face. But his character lacked serious-
ness or self-control. He was superficial, ostentatious,
and sometimes dissolute. But many people are fascinated
by depravity and disinclined for austere morals on the
throne. Such men found Piso's qualities attractive.

However, his ambitions were not what originated the conspiracy. Who did, who initiated the enterprise which so many joined, I could not easily say. Subrius Flavus, a colonel of the Guard, and Sulpicius Asper, company-commander, were in the forefront – as their courageous deaths showed. Violent hatred was what brought in Lucan and Plautius Lateranus. Lucan's animosity was personal. For Nero had the impudence to compete with Lucan as a poet, and had impeded his reputation by vetoing his publicity. Lateranus joined from no personal grievance; his motive was patriotism. Two other senators, Flavius Scaevinus and Afranius Quintianus, belied their reputations by becoming leaders in so important a project. For Scaevinus' brain was ruined by dissipation, and he led a languid sleepy life. Quintianus was a notorious degenerate who had been insulted by Nero in an offensive poem, and desired revenge.

These men talked to each other, and to their friends, about the emperor's crimes and his reign's imminent close. They were joined by seven Roman knights: Claudius Senecio, Cervarius Proculus, Volcacius Araricus, Julius Augurinus, Munatius Gratus, Antonius Natalis, and Marcius Festus. Senecio was Nero's close associate, and so his position was especially perilous since they were still ostensibly friends. Natalis shared all Piso's secrets. The rest looked to revolution for personal advancement. Nor were Flavus and Asper the only officers involved. Other accomplices were the Guard colonels, Gaius Gavius Silvanus and Statius Proxumus, and company-commanders, Maximus Scaurus and Venetus Paulus, were also in the plot. But the mainstay was felt to be Faenius Rufus, commander of the Guard. His respectability and good reputation had made less impression on Nero than the cruelty and depravity of his colleague Tigellinus – who persecuted Faenius with slanders, reiterating the alarming allegation that he had been Agrippina's lover and was intent on avenging her.

So when the conspirators were satisfied by Faenius' own repeated assurances that he was with them, serious discussion began about the date and place of Nero's murder. Subrius Flavus, it was said, had felt tempted to attack Nero when the emperor was singing on the stage or rushing from place to place during the night, unguarded, while his palace burned. Flavus had been attracted to the latter instance by Nero's opportune solitude, and in the former, conversely, by the large crowds which would witness the noble deed. But what held him back was that hindrance to all mighty enterprises, the desire for survival.

The plotters hesitated, still hoping and fearing. A woman called Epicharis, who had extracted their secret – it is not known how, for she had never before interested herself in anything good – kept urging them on and assailing them. Finally, happening to be in Campania and becoming impatient with the slowness of the conspirators, she attempted to unsettle and implicate the naval officers at Misenum. She began with a rear-admiral named Volusius Proculus, who had helped Nero with his mother's murder and felt his promotion had fallen short of so tremendous a crime. Whether their friendship was longstanding or recent is unknown. At all events Proculus told the woman of his services to Nero and their inadequate reward, and expressed not only discontent but the determination to have his own back if the chance occurred. This raised hopes that Proculus might be induced to act, and bring others in. The fleet could be extremely useful and provide valuable opportunities, since Nero enjoyed going to sea off Puteoli and Misenum.

So Epicharis went further. Enlarging on the emperor's abolition of the senate's rights and whole criminal record, she revealed the plan to avenge Rome's destruction at Nero's hands – only let Proculus make ready to do his part by winning over the best men, and he should be worthily rewarded. But she did not disclose the names of the conspirators. So, when Proculus proceeded – as he did – to report what he had heard to Nero, his information was useless. Epicharis was summoned and confronted with Proculus, but in the absence of witnesses easily refuted him. However, she herself was kept in custody. For Nero suspected that the story, though unproven, might not be untrue.

The conspirators were now tormented by fears of betrayal. They wanted to perform the assassination quickly – at Piso's villa at Baiae. For Nero appreciated its charms and often came for a bathe or banquet, without guards or imperial pomp. But Piso refused, arguing that to stain the sanctity of hospitality with the blood of an emperor, however evil, would cause a bad impression. The city would be a better place, he said – that detested palace Nero had plundered his people to build; or, since their deed would be in the public interest, a public centre.

That was what Piso said aloud. But secretly he was afraid of a rival claimant to the throne – Lucius Silanus Torquatus (II). The illustrious birth of Torquatus, and his upbringing by Gaius Cassius Longinus, fitted him for the highest destiny. Moreover non-conspirators, who might pity Nero as the victim of a crime, would back Torquatus readily. Some thought that Piso had also wished to prevent the lively consul, Marcus Julius Vestinus Atticus, from leading a Republican movement or insisting that the next emperor should be chosen by himself. For Vestinus was not one of the conspirators – though Nero used the charge to gratify his longstanding hatred of an innocent man.

They finally decided to execute their design at the Circus Games, on the day dedicated to Ceres. For though Nero rarely left the seclusion of his palace and gardens, he often attended Circus performances, and was more accessible in their festive atmosphere. The attack was planned as follows. Plautius Lateranus, ostensibly petitioning for financial assistance, was to prostrate himself before the unsuspecting emperor and then – being both resolute and muscular – bring him down and hold him. As Nero lay pinned down, the military men among the plotters, and any others sufficiently daring, would rush up and kill him. The leading role was claimed by Flavius Scaevinus, who had taken a dagger from a temple of Safety or (according to other reports) from the Shrine of Fortune at Ferentum, and wore it as the dedicated instrument of a great enterprise.

Meanwhile Piso was to wait at the temple of Ceres, from which Faenius Rufus and the rest were to fetch him to the Guards' camp. The elder Pliny adds that, to win popular favour for Piso, Claudius' daughter Claudia Antonia was to accompany him. True or false, I have felt that this statement ought at least to be recorded. Yet it seems absurd either that Claudia Antonia should have staked her name and life on so hopeless a project, or that Piso, famous for his devotion to his wife, could have pledged himself to another marriage – unless indeed the lust for power outblazes all other feelings combined.

The secret was astonishingly well kept, considering the differences of the conspirators in social and financial position, rank, age, and sex. But betrayal came in the end – from the house of Flavius Scaevinus. The day before the attempt, he had a long conversation with Antonius Natalis. Then Scaevinus returned home and signed his will. Taking the aforesaid dagger from its sheath, and complaining that it was blunt with age, he gave it to his freed slave Milichus to be sharpened and polished on a stone. Then came a dinner-party, more luxurious than usual, at which Scaevinus freed his favourite slaves and gave others presents of money. He maintained a desultory conversation with superficial gaiety. But he was evidently anxious and seriously pre-occupied. Finally, he instructed the same Milichus to prepare bandages and styptics for wounds.

Perhaps Milichus was in the secret, and had hitherto proved trustworthy. Alternatively (and this is the usual version) he knew nothing, but his suspicions were now aroused. At all events his slave's brain considered the rewards of treachery and conceived ideas of vast wealth and power. Then morality, his patron's life, gratitude for his freedom, counted for nothing. His wife's womanly, sordid advice implanted a further motive, fear. Many slaves and former slaves, she recalled, had been there and seen the same happenings – one man's silence would be useless, and the rewards would go to the informer who spoke first.

So at daybreak Milichus left for the Servilian Gardens. At first he was kept out. Finally, however, after insisting on the dreadful gravity of his news, he was taken by the doorkeepers to Nero's freed slave Epaphroditus – who conducted him to Nero. Milichus then revealed the resolute determination of the senators, the danger to Nero's life, and everything else he had heard or guessed. Exhibiting the dagger destined for Nero's murder,

Milichus urged that the accused man be fetched. Scaevinus was arrested by soldiers. But he denied his guilt.

'The weapon concerned in the charge', he said 'is a venerated heirloom kept in my bedroom. This ex-slave Milichus has stolen it. As to my will, I have often signed new clauses without particularly noting the date. I have given slaves their freedom and money-gifts before. This time the scale was larger because, with reduced means and pressing creditors, I feared my will would be rejected. My table has always been generous, my life comfortable – too comfortable for austere critics. Bandages for wounds I did not order. But the man's allegations of patent untruths are so unconvincing that he has added this charge merely because it rests wholly on his own evidence.'

Scaevinus spiritedly reinforced this defence by assailing the ex-slave as an infamous rascal. His self-possessed tones and features would have annihilated the accusation if Milichus' wife had not reminded her husband that Scaevinus had spoken privately and at length with Antonius Natalis, and that both of them were associates of Gaius Calpurnius Piso. So Natalis was summoned, and he and Scaevinus were interrogated separately about their conversation and its subject. The discrepancy between their replies aroused suspicion, and they were put in chains.

At the threat and sight of torture they broke down – Natalis first. With his more intimate knowledge of the whole conspiracy (and greater cunning as an accuser), he began by denouncing Piso – then Seneca. Either Natalis had really acted as intermediary between Seneca and Piso or he hoped to conciliate Nero, who loathed Seneca and sought every means to destroy him. Scaevinus was equally unheroic – or he may have thought that since all was known silence held no advantages. At all events, when told of Natalis' confession, he named the remaining conspirators. Of these, Lucan, Afranius Quintianus, and Claudius Senecio long refused to incriminate themselves. But finally, tempted by a bribe of impunity, they confessed. What they said explained their hesitation, for Lucan denounced his own mother, Acilia, and his two partners implicated their closest friends, Glitius Gallus and Annius Pollio.

Nero now remembered the information of Volusius Proculus and consequent arrest of Epicharis. Thinking no female body could stand the pain, he ordered her to be tortured. But lashes did not weaken her denials, nor did branding – nor the fury of the torturers at being defied by a woman. So the first day's examination was frustrated. Next day her racked limbs could not support her, so she was taken for further torments in a chair. But on the way she tore off her breast-band, and fastened it in a noose to the chair's canopy, and placed her neck inside it. Then, straining with all her weight, she throttled the little life that was still in her. So, shielding in direst agony men unconnected with her and almost strangers, this former slavewoman set an example which particularly shone when free men, Roman knights and senators, were betraying, before anybody had laid a hand on them, their nearest and dearest. For Lucan and Senecio and Quintianus gave away their fellow-conspirators wholesale.

Nero became increasingly frightened. His guard had been redoubled. Indeed, the whole of Rome was virtually put in custody – troops manned the walls, and blockaded the city by sea and river. Roman public squares and homes, and even neighbouring towns and country districts, were invaded by infantry and cavalry. Among them were Germans; being foreigners, the emperor trusted them particularly.

Line after line of chained men were dragged to their

destination at the gates of Nero's Gardens. When they were brought in to be interrogated, guilt was deduced from affability to a conspirator, or a chance conversation or meeting, or entrance to a party or a show together. Fierce interrogation by Nero and Tigellinus was supplemented by savage attacks from Faenius Rufus. No informer had denounced him yet; so, to establish his independence of his fellow-conspirators, he bullied them. When Subrius Flavius, who was standing by, inquired by a sign – in the middle of an actual trial – if he should draw his sword and assassinate Nero, Faenius Rufus shook his head and checked Subrius' impulse as his hand was already moving to the hilt.

After the betrayal of the plot, while Milichus was talking and Scaevinus hesitating, Piso was urged to go to the Guards' camp and test the attitude of the troops, or mount the platform in the Forum and try the civilians. 'If your fellow-conspirators rally round you', it was argued, 'outsiders will follow. Once a move is made the publicity will be immense – a vitally important point in revolutions. Nero has taken no precautions against this. Unforeseen developments intimidate even courageous men, so how could forcible counter-measures be feared from this actor – with Tigellinus and Tigellinus' mistresses as his escort! Many things that look hard to timid people can be done by trying.

'It is useless to expect loyal silence when so many accomplices are involved, body and soul. Tortures and rewards find a way anywhere. You too will be visited and put in chains – and ultimately to a degrading death. How much finer to die for the good of your country, calling for men to defend its freedom! The army may fail you, the people abandon you. But you yourself – if you must die early – die in a way of which your ancestors and posterity could approve!'

But Piso was unimpressed. After a brief public appearance, he shut himself in his house and summoned up courage for his end, waiting for the Guardsmen. Nero, suspicious of old soldiers as likely supporters of Piso, had selected new or recent recruits as his assassins. But Piso died by opening the veins in his arms. He loaded his will with repulsive flattery of Nero. This was done because Piso loved his own wife, Satria Galla, though she was low-born and her beauty her only asset. He had stolen her from her former husband, a friend of his called Domitius Silus, whose complaisance – like her misconduct – had increased Piso's notoriety.

The next to be killed by Nero was the consul-designate Plautius Lateranus. His removal was so hasty that he was not allowed to embrace his children or given the customary short respite to choose his own death. Hurried off to the place reserved for slaves' executions, Lateranus was dispatched by a Guard colonel, Statius Proxumus. He died in resolute silence – without denouncing the officer's equal guilt.

Seneca's death followed. It delighted the emperor. Nero had no proof of Seneca's complicity but was glad to use arms against him when poison had failed. The only evidence was a statement of Antonius Natalis that he had been sent to visit the ailing Seneca and complain because Seneca had refused to receive Piso. Natalis had conveyed the message that friends ought to have friendly meetings; and Seneca had answered that frequent meetings and conversations would benefit neither: but that his own welfare depended on Piso's.

A colonel of the Guard, Gavius Silvanus, was ordered to convey this report to Seneca and ask whether he admitted that those were the words of Natalis and himself. Fortuitously or intentionally, Seneca had returned that day from Campania and halted at a villa four miles from Rome. Towards evening the officer arrived. Surrounding the villa with pickets, he delivered the emperor's message to Seneca as he dined with his wife, Pompeia Paulina, and two friends. Seneca replied as follows: 'Natalis was sent to me to protest, on Piso's behalf, because I would not let him visit me. I answered excusing myself on grounds of health and love of quiet. I could have had no reason to value any private person's welfare above my own. Nor am I a flatterer. Nero knows this exceptionally well. He has had more frankness than servility from Seneca!'

The officer reported this to Nero in the presence of Poppaea and Tigellinus, intimate counsellors of the emperor's brutalities. Nero asked if Seneca was preparing for suicide. Gavius Silvanus replied that he had noticed no sign of fear or sadness in his words or features. So Silvanus was ordered to go back and notify the death-sentence. According to Fabius Rusticus, he did not return by the way he had come but made a detour to visit the commander of the Guard, Faenius Rufus; he showed Faenius the emperor's orders, asking if he should obey them; and Faenius, with that ineluctable weakness which they all revealed, told him to obey. For Silvanus was himself one of the conspirators – and now he was adding to the crimes which he had conspired to avenge. But he shirked communicating or witnessing the atrocity. Instead he sent in one of his staff-officers to tell Seneca he must die.

Unperturbed, Seneca asked for his will. But the officer refused. Then Seneca turned to his friends. 'Being forbidden', he said, 'to show gratitude for your services, I leave you my one remaining possession, and my best: the pattern of my life. If you remember it, your devoted friendship will be rewarded by a name for virtuous accomplishments.' As he talked – and sometimes in sterner and more imperative terms – he checked their tears and sought to revive their courage. Where had their philosophy gone, he asked, and that resolution against impending misfortunes which they had devised over so many years? 'Surely nobody was unaware that Nero was cruel!' he added. 'After murdering his mother and brother, it only remained for him to kill his teacher and tutor.'

These words were evidently intended for public hearing. Then Seneca embraced his wife and, with a tenderness very different from his philosophical imperturbability, entreated her to moderate and set a term for her grief, and take just consolation, in her bereavement, from contemplating his well-spent life. Nevertheless, she insisted on dying with him, and demanded the executioner's stroke. Seneca did not oppose her brave decision. Indeed, loving her wholeheartedly, he was reluctant to leave her behind to be persecuted. 'Solace in life was what I commended to you,' he said. 'But you prefer death and glory. I will not grudge your setting so fine an example. We can die with equal fortitude. But yours will be the nobler end.'

Then, each with one incision of the blade, he and his wife cut their arms. But Seneca's aged body, lean from austere living, released the blood too slowly. So he also severed the veins in his ankles and behind his knees. Exhausted by severe pain, he was afraid of weakening his wife's endurance by betraying his agony – or of losing his own self-possession at the sight of her sufferings. So he asked her to go into another bedroom. But even in his last moments his eloquence remained. Summoning secretaries, he dictated a dissertation. (It has been published in his own words, so I shall refrain from paraphrasing it.)

Nero did not dislike Paulina personally. In order, therefore, to avoid increasing his ill-repute for cruelty, he ordered her suicide to be averted. So, on instructions from the soldiers, slaves and ex-slaves bandaged her arm and stopped the bleeding. She may have been unconscious. But discreditable versions are always popular, and some took a different view – that as long as she feared there was no appeasing Nero, she coveted the distinction of dying with her husband, but when better prospects appeared life's attractions got the better of her. She lived on for a few years, honourably loyal to her husband's memory, with pallid features and limbs which showed how much vital blood she had lost.

Meanwhile Seneca's death was slow and lingering. Poison, such as was formerly used to execute State criminals at Athens, had long been prepared; and Seneca now entreated his experienced doctor, Annaeus Statius, who was also an old friend, to supply it. But when it came, Seneca drank it without effect. For his limbs were already cold and numbed against the poison's action. Finally he was placed in a bath of warm water. He sprinkled a little of it on the attendant slaves, commenting that it was a libation to Jupiter. Then he was carried into a vapour-bath, where he suffocated. His cremation was without ceremony, in accordance with his own instructions about his death – written at the height of his wealth and power.

It was rumoured that Subrius Flavus and certain company-commanders of the Guard had secretly plotted, with Seneca's knowledge, that when Nero had been killed by Piso's agency Piso too should be murdered, and the throne given to Seneca: it would look as though men uninvolved in the plot had chosen Seneca for his moral qualities. Flavus was widely quoted as saying that, in point of disgrace, it made little difference to remove a lyre-player and replace him by a performer of tragedies. For Nero's singing to the lyre was paralleled by Piso's singing of tragic parts.

But the respite of the army conspirators was at an end. Finding Faenius Rufus' dual role as plotter and inquisitor intolerable, those who had turned informers longed to betray him. So while he pressed and threatened Scaevinus the latter retorted sneeringly that no one was better informed than Faenius himself – he should demonstrate his gratitude voluntarily to his excellent emperor. Words failed Faenius in reply. So did silence; a stammering utterance betrayed his terror. The remaining conspirators, especially the knight Cervarius Proculus, pressed for his conviction. The emperor ordered a soldier named Cassius, who was in attendance because of his great physical strength, to seize Faenius and bind him.

The evidence of the same fellow-conspirators next

destroyed the Guard colonel Subrius Flavus. His first line of defence was difference of character: a soldier like him would never have shared such an enterprise with these effeminate civilians. But, when pressed, Flavus admitted his guilt, and gloried in it. Asked by Nero why he had forgotten his military oath, he replied: 'Because I detested you! I was as loyal as any of your soldiers as long as you deserved affection. I began detesting you when you murdered your mother and wife and became charioteer, actor, and incendiary!' I have given his actual words because they did not obtain the publicity of Seneca's; yet the soldier's blunt, forceful utterance was equally worth recording. Nothing in this conspiracy fell more shockingly on Nero's ears. For although ready enough to commit crimes, he was unaccustomed to be told about them.

A fellow-colonel, Veianius Niger, was detailed to execute Flavus. But when he ordered a grave to be dug in a field nearby, Flavus objected it was too shallow and narrow. 'More bad discipline,' he remarked to the soldiers in attendance. Then, bidden to offer his neck firmly, he replied: 'You strike equally firmly!' But the executioner, trembling violently, only just severed the head with two blows. However, he boasted of his ferocity to Nero, saying he had killed Flavus with 'a stroke and a half!'

Another officer of the Guard, the company-commander Sulpicius Asper, was the next to show exemplary courage. For when Nero asked why he planned to kill him, Asper replied that it was the only way to rescue Nero from evil ways. He was convicted and executed. His equals likewise died without disgracing themselves. But Faenius Rufus was less brave – and could not keep lamentations even out of his will.

Nero was also expecting the incrimination of the consul Marcus Julius Vestinus Atticus, whom he regarded as revolutionary and disaffected. But none of the conspirators had confided in Vestinus. Some had long-standing feuds with him; others thought him impetuous and independent. Nero hated him as a result of their intimate association. For Vestinus knew and despised the emperor's worthlessness, while Nero feared his outspoken friend, who made him the butt of crude jokes; when they are based on truth, they rankle. Besides, Vestinus had added a further motive by marrying Statilia Messalina, although he knew her to be one of Nero's mistresses. Yet no accuser came forward, and there was no charge.

So Nero could not assume the judge's role. Accordingly, he behaved like an aristocrat instead, and sent a battalion of the Guard. Its commander, Gerellanus, was ordered to forestall the consul's designs, seize his 'citadel', and overpower his picked young followers. For the house where Vestinus lived overlooked the Forum, and he kept handsome slaves, all young. Vestinus had finished his consular duties for the day and was giving a dinner-party – unsuspecting, or pretending to be – when the soldiers entered and said the commander wanted him. He instantly rose and rapidly initiated all his arrangements. Shutting himself in his bedroom, he called his doctor and had his veins cut. Before the effects were felt, he was carried to a vapour-bath, and plunged into hot water. No word of self-pity escaped him. Meanwhile his dinner-companions were surrounded by Guardsmen and not released until late at night. It amused Nero to picture their expectation of death after dinner. But finally he ruled that they had been punished enough for their consular party.

Then he ordered Lucan to die. When he felt loss of blood numbing his feet and hands, and life gradually leaving his extremities (though his heart was still warm, and his brain clear), Lucan remembered verses he had written about a wounded soldier who had died a similar death. His last words were a recitation of this passage. Claudius Senecio, Afranius Quintianus, and Flavius Scaevinus were the next to die. Their deaths belied their effeminate lives. Then, without memorable words or actions, the remaining conspirators perished.

Executions now abounded in the city, and thank-offerings on the Capitol. Men who had lost their sons, or brothers, or other kinsmen, or friends, thanked the gods and decorated their houses with laurel, and fell before Nero, kissing his hand incessantly.

PENGUIN 60s CLASSICS

PENGUIN 60s CLASSICS

ANONYMOUS WORKS